STANLEY TIMBRE

How To Stop Overthinking After Being Cheated On

This book was professionally typeset on Reedsy.
Find out more at reedsy.com

Contents

INTRODUCTION

When you first meet someone and begin a new relationship, the last thing on your mind is that they might even consider cheating on you. However, whether you are married or in a long-term healthy relationship, you only learn that the person you love has been unfaithful after you have been together for a while.

Whether it involves an emotional or a physical affair, cheating is unquestionably one of the most trying times that any relationship can go through. You undoubtedly feel saddened, angry, and worried if you've just learned that your spouse is having an extramarital affair. You only desire an end to the pain so that your broken heart can begin to mend. If these unpleasant emotions aren't properly addressed, they might influence you to make rash decisions that have an impact on your relationships and quality of life.

When you are the victim of an unfaithful lover, you must decide whether to stay or leave. Knowing when to move away is the hardest reality to accept after learning of your spouse's infidelity. This is in addition to the unpleasant feelings you feel. It's normal to feel confused when a tornado of emotions hits.

Most people struggle to decide whether to get a divorce, end a relationship, or continue having an affair. Most people's initial concern is whether infidelity can survive in marriage.

One

How to Avoid Thinking Too Much in a Relationship

~⚬✦⚬~

Rumination, sometimes referred to as overthinking, is a frequent occurrence. People often overthink certain issues. You or your partner could tend to overthink the relationship whether you're in a romantic relationship, whether you've been dating for a short while, it's been a while, or even if you're already married.

Although this is a typical occurrence, your relationship may be in danger. How then can you deal with this propensity or practice of yours? Just relax. You may learn how to quit overanalyzing relationships by reading this book.

Overthinking your spouse or the course of your relationship may begin as a passing thought. The problem is that it may become a habit. So read on to find out how to quit over analyzing relationships.

You'll discover the causes of people's propensity to overthink relationships and their partners as well as how it could affect your love partnership. The book also offers suggestions for avoiding relationship over analysis.

Why do individuals second-guess themselves in relationships?

To better understand a habit or problem, it is a good idea to investigate its origins. This also holds for overthinking. Knowing why you're even thinking is the greatest method to cope with overthinking.

You may be able to identify the kinds of methods that can help you break your habit of ruminating if you can identify the cause of it.

Then why do individuals second-guess themselves, particularly in relationships?

One typical explanation is that you may be experiencing relationship insecurity.

The problem is that this uneasiness might have two separate causes: first, unsatisfactory prior romantic encounters, and second, low self-esteem.

Anxiety could also be a factor. Anxiety and overthinking go hand in hand. If you tend to be high-strung and worried in general, your relationship may also reflect it.

Another reason you could wonder whether your spouse loves you or not is a lack of understanding of your and their respective love languages. Each person has a favorite love language. There are several varieties of love languages.

Why is relationship overthinking such a major issue?

Now that you are aware of several important reasons for overthinking. Additionally, you are aware that overthinking is a prevalent phenomenon among many individuals. As a result, you may naturally ask whether it is harmful and, if so, why.

Your mental health and how you feel may both be negatively impacted by overthinking. You can start nitpicking if you overthink your partnership and your connection. This nitpicking might cause you to see issues when none exist. When you overthink a situation, you begin making up problems for your relationship in your thoughts and are more likely to criticize your partner, spouse, girlfriend, or boyfriend. Overall, you could experience stress and misery. Therefore, this self-limiting problem might harm your mental health.

Let's now discuss ways to avoid overthinking in relationships;

1. Attempt to be active and productive

Overthinking tendencies often worsen when one's potential for productivity isn't fully realized. Being productive goes beyond just being occupied at work. You may also make an effort to continue working by improving your connection. Maybe you can arrange a lovely date night and make it happen! Plan a pleasant trek with your lover if you both want to go hiking. These are but a few instances.

2. Making a life for yourself outside of your partnership

Having many areas of attention in your life might be a fantastic strategy to combat your propensity for overthinking. Your personal and professional lives are affected by this. Take up an activity that you haven't engaged in recently!

Have you been meaning to do a fun project but haven't yet? The moment is now to act!

3. Interact with your loved ones and friends.

Every person's life revolves around their friends and family. Your family and friends were in your life even when you hadn't found your soul mate. Decide on a regular time to spend with your family, friends, and other loved ones.

You can also get the chance to discuss your worries and other topics when you meet up with your close friends and loved ones.

4. Develop an evidence-based way of thinking.

People who often experience anxiety should pay particular attention to this issue. So do you overthink when you're anxious?

Yes, to put it. People experience anxiety when they look forward to upcoming occurrences. Rumination and this tendency go hand in hand.

However, if you give it too much thought, you're simply speculating. Is there any proof to back up your theory? It is preferable to take an evidence-based approach to this scenario if there is no proof to back up your beliefs about your connection.

5. Don't personalize everything

If you notice that your girlfriend or boyfriend is upset, there may be several unrelated factors at play. Perhaps they had a stressful day at work or had a negative interaction with someone.

It's not always true that you were to blame for someone else's poor mood just because they are in one. Therefore, rather than putting yourself through the agony of overthinking things, it could be preferable to ask them what occurred.

Two

How to Quit Overthinking After a Cheating Relationship

fter being cheated on, it's normal to feel betrayed, uneasy, and overwhelmed. It might be common to find oneself going over certain events or dissecting particular actions, but doing so can also result in worry and chronic overthinking. Fortunately, there are several strategies for putting an end to overthinking after being duped and creating strong, lasting bonds.

Why Do I Think Too Much Now That I've Been Cheated On?

Overthinking is a word that most of us have heard of and even used. While we may not think it is all that awful, it may cause us to conclude without any solid supporting data. It is normal for the partner who was betrayed in a relationship to overthink because they may be preoccupied with the possibility that it can happen again, which can lead to issues with self-esteem and trust. When your spouse goes out, spends too much time on their phone, or modifies certain rituals, you may worry.

Overthinking may occur more often and with greater intensity after infidelity for those who struggle with OCD, anxiety, or other mood problems.

Following adultery, some causes of overthinking include:

- a low sense of self
- Disorder of compulsive behavior
- Anxiety\sDepression
- trauma-related stress disorder
- abusive relationships in the past
- Prior partnerships with infidelity

Effects of Adultery

Overthinking is a common side effect of adultery and may also signify more serious consequences of betrayal, such as anxiety and infidelity PTSD. Grief and loss-related emotions, trauma brain, and heightened toxic stress are additional impacts.

Following infidelity, those who battle with overthinking may also have:

Relationship phobia

After infidelity, it is typical to suffer relationship anxiety, which may be either the cause or a symptom of overthinking. This will undoubtedly result in some relationship anxiety and bothersome ideas about a spouse who is cheating—or even prospective partners who have no history of infidelity.

Adultery PTSD

Overanalyzing following adultery is often a sign of PTSD related to infidelity. The individual who was betrayed may have long-lasting betrayal trauma as a result of the adultery after it has occurred. Making and keeping good relationships may be challenging for those with this kind of PTSD.

OCD in relationships:

As individuals might get fixated on averting future affairs, relationship OCD can cause and/or result in intrusive thoughts and overthinking. To deal with their concerns, they could become fixated on their relationship and constantly evaluate their present and potential romantic interests.

PTSD in relationships:

Similar to infidelity PTSD, relationship PTSD is a more general phrase that also encompasses cases of physical or emotional abuse, trauma bonding, and other betrayals.

Paranoia:

Overthinking often causes paranoia because it allows your mind to wander without any boundaries, enabling you to indulge in paranoid ideas and anxieties.

Fifteen (15) Strategies To Help You Avoid Overthinking After Being Cheated On

The following will help you avoid overthinking after being cheated on;

1. Discover the cause of your overthinking

It's crucial to consider carefully why you overthink. After adultery, it could seem like a no-brainer question, but overthinking can also be caused by underlying issues or a trauma reaction in progress. You may learn how to quit overthinking by grasping the details.

2. Rely on interpersonal aid

When you're feeling low, rely on your friends and family for support. When you are going through a tough moment, particularly when you are trying to regain your confidence and sense of worth after a toxic relationship, social support is crucial.

3. Address issues with trust

Rebuilding trust in your relationship is crucial to accomplish if you decide to remain together since trust difficulties are common after suffering any kind of betrayal, including adultery. This often entails working on any trust problems you may have since you could have trouble feeling secure in your perception and judgment. Making a place where you may openly communicate, express your thoughts, and be heard is crucial. It might be difficult to know where to begin.

4. Engage in mindfulness

The symptoms of anxiety, stress, depression, PTSD, and emotional reactivity may be lessened by mindfulness. Try to keep an awareness of your surroundings and concentrate on the things you can manage right now. When you feel overwhelmed, calm down, use relaxation methods, and take things one day at a time.

5. Examine a New Setting

Giving yourself a setting that makes you feel like you're starting over will assist you in entering a different frame of mind and open the door to more effective coping strategies. This environment shift might be dramatic, like moving to a new home or going on a long trip, or it can be subtle, like moving furniture about in your home.

6. Recognition

Accepting that there has been adultery and betrayal in your relationship might seem difficult, if not impossible. Because it requires letting go of the hurt of betrayal and learning to live with it, acceptance is often challenging. This is often likened to the grieving process' acceptance phase.

7. Improve Yourself

A person's capacity to take care of oneself may be negatively impacted by the insecurities, despair, and anxiety that often follow adultery. Healing requires time spent on self-care and finding methods to feel more at ease in your skin. Remember to be patient since it may take some time to reestablish your values and priorities following infidelity. Physical self-care is often essential to practice emotional self-care as well.

8. Confidence in Oneself

A little self-love and encouraging words may go a long way. Overanalyzing and intrusive thoughts often result in negative self-talk and pessimism, both of which may worsen your mental health. Giving oneself love and encouraging words is very essential. Even while it may seem strange to begin telling oneself these things, doing so may greatly help you in your emotional recovery and regulation.

9. Cease Worrying About What-Ifs

It might be difficult to let go when you go through all the hypotheticals and consider every concept in detail. Although there is nothing that can be done to reverse what has occurred, it might be difficult to quit thinking excessively about someone or something that has caused significant pain. This can result in disordered thinking. To reduce thought spirals concerning infidelity, it might be extremely beneficial to learn how to practice thought pausing.

10. Journaling.

By expressing what you are feeling and how you are coping, journaling may help you control your overthinking and enhance your mental health. Rereading your writing from time to time might be useful for boosting your confidence and reflecting on how things have changed.

11. Yoga

Yoga gives you something to concentrate on, which, like journaling and mindfulness, may help you reduce anxiety and slow down your thoughts. Yoga also aids in breathing in harmony with movement and cultivates a more conscious way of being via breathwork.

12. Take an active step

Playing a sport or exercising may make you feel better mentally and can help you focus on the task at hand instead of overanalyzing it. It may give you a change of pace, help you concentrate on your breathing, and help you control your emotions. While some people find it challenging to exercise while their minds are racing, others find that it improves their sleep and reduces stress. Going outside to enjoy nature might help your mental health, yet it might not be everyone's best coping mechanism. You may check how you feel by taking a bike ride, a run in your neighborhood, or a stroll around the park.

13. Produce an item

It may be beneficial to express your feelings via art, such as painting, drawing, ceramics, or anything else that enables you to do so. People who are suffering from trauma may benefit from expressive arts therapy and art therapy.

14. Be a Part of a Support Group

When handling infidelity, support groups are excellent for those who desire or need a stronger feeling of community. To feel less alone, you may find it extremely beneficial to discover a community of others going through infidelity rehabilitation. Support groups provide you with the environment and people where it may be safe to express your emotions. Overthinking can be an isolating experience.

15. Create fresh routines

Your mind may concentrate on developing new, constructive neural connections when you establish new patterns. When you're dealing with uncertainty, poor self-esteem, depression, and/or anxiety, starting anything new may be difficult. That's why incorporating your social and personal support networks may be particularly beneficial.

How Does Therapy Work?

Overthinking may be an indication of a more serious problem, therefore it's crucial to think about speaking with a professional about your symptoms and current pressures to learn how to control your negative thoughts. If left unchecked, overthinking may develop into other problems that are more difficult to handle.

Finding the proper therapist may assist with coping skill development, managing anxiety, overthinking, tension, and working through depressive and insecure emotions. Marriage and couples therapy might assist your relationship after infidelity whether you decide to remain together or have trouble starting new relationships. Asking friends and family or other health care providers, such as your primary care physician, is one approach to discovering a therapist. However, browsing an online therapist directory is a fantastic way to filter for particular qualities you are looking for in a therapist.

Final Reflections

After being duped, overthinking might seem tough to overcome, but you are not the only one who experiences this. Fortunately, there are several methods you can use to stop overanalyzing, reclaim your confidence and self-esteem, and reestablish your trust in other people and yourself.

Three

How to Stop Having Bad Thoughts in a Relationship

A strong relationship may be ruined by a variety of factors. Even though adultery may be the first thing that comes to mind, psychologists claim that negative or excessive thinking is more likely to destroy a relationship than anything else. Recognize your harmful patterns and routines, such as negative thinking, if you want to keep your relationship healthy. People who suffer from anxiety and depression often have negative thinking patterns, which may seriously damage a relationship. It's normal to sometimes worry while you're in a relationship. Thoughts such as, "Nothing ever works out for me," "My ex cheated on me, so he will too," or "We'll just end up breaking up anyhow" are examples of negative thinking.

How to Let Go of Unfavorable Thought Patterns in a Relationship

Finding techniques to transform negative ideas into good ones is crucial. You will constantly anticipate the worst of your relationship if you enter each one believing that your spouse would break up with you or be unfaithful. Here are some strategies you may use to break negative thought patterns in your relationship:

1. Live in the present and let the past go: You could find it tough to let go of the past and move on if you've been injured in relationships in the past. This is often brought on by a desire to keep from being wounded in a new relationship. You are damaging a new relationship if you bring up problems from previous relationships. It is easier said than done, but to move on, you must let go of any previous pain.

2. Discover new energy-channeling strategies: You may act irrationally as a result of negative thoughts, such as going through your partner's phone or believing you are unworthy of them. It would be a good idea to discover other methods to channel these thoughts if you are continually seeking confirmation and reassurance that your spouse still cares. Take some time for yourself if you see yourself slipping into these destructive mental patterns. Focus your attention on a pastime, a stroll, some breathing exercises, or a book.

3. Never assume anything: The idea that we know what our spouse is thinking might lead to negative mental habits. Never make hasty judgments. Instead, make an effort to clarify things with your spouse via communication.

4. Tell someone one thing: We all engage in it. We talk to other individuals when we are angry or irritated. However, if you are complaining to lots of

people about how your relationship is making you feel, it may encourage more negativity and change how other people see your partner. Choose one dependable person instead to confide in when a problem develops.

5. Make a note of the unfavorable thinking patterns you have: Make a note of all the negative thinking patterns you are experiencing as a helpful practice. Write a potentially good outcome next to each negative thinking pattern. Write it down, for instance, if your significant other is taking longer than usual to reply to your text and it is upsetting you. Write down every possible explanation for why they could be taking so long to react, such as they are busy, they are asleep, etc., next to the negative notion.

6. Keep in mind that both you and your relationship are flawed since we are all just human: Everybody has flaws and makes errors. Your spouse won't always act morally. It's a good idea to have a positive outlook on the relationship when you are disappointed with your mate. Instead, let them know what you need and how their behavior is making you feel.

7. Don't take things personally too much: Even the most fulfilling relationships go through ups and downs. Sometimes having a conversation may be difficult. Take advantage of the ups and downs and learn from them. Healthy thinking helps lessen the signs of anxiety and despair. Worry and terror might rise when we think negatively. Healthy thinking will ultimately come naturally to you if you consistently practice it. Healthy thinking may not, however, be sufficient on its own to lessen anxiety and despair. It's crucial to get in touch with a certified anxiety therapist or depression therapist if thoughts start to seem too overpowering.

Four

How To Direct Your Energy To Control What You Can't Control

Focusing on the things we are unable to change makes it simple to feel trapped in a rut. We are indeed more prone to experience anxiety, rage, and disappointment the more we concentrate on factors beyond our control. In contrast, we may experience happiness, confidence, empowerment, and a feeling of accomplishment when we concentrate on what we can control. But how can we tell what is within our control and what is not?

We shall investigate in this piece if we have any influence over our emotions and ideas. How? We will examine the negative effects of controlling ideas and emotions as well as strategies for dealing with impossibilities. We'll look at techniques based on mindfulness training to help you become more adept at exerting control over the things you can.

Focusing on the things we are unable to change makes it simple to feel trapped in a rut. We are indeed more prone to experience anxiety, rage, and disappointment the more we concentrate on factors beyond our control. In contrast, we may experience happiness, confidence, empowerment, and a feeling of accomplishment when we concentrate on what we can control. But how can we tell what is within our control and what is not?

We shall investigate in this piece if we have any influence over our emotions and ideas. How? We will examine the negative effects of controlling ideas and emotions as well as strategies for dealing with impossibilities. We'll look at techniques based on mindfulness training to help you become more adept at exerting control over the things you can.

What can we control?

You may start to give yourself some leeway for having certain emotions and telling yourself these are out of your control now that you've dispelled the notion that you have complete control over your thoughts and feelings. You have more energy to pay attention to tough thoughts and emotions when you let go of the idea that you can control and suppress them. We have some influence over this. We do have control over how we react to our ideas and emotions. To do this, we must make the effort to become aware of how our ideas and emotions are affecting us and take action to change this course.

The first step in empowering yourself and redirecting your attention to those things that you can control is realizing what you can and cannot manage.

Being conscious might help you take back control. Being present, self-aware, and involved in what you are doing and where you are at that time is the practice of mindfulness. When we practice mindfulness, we develop the attentional skill of seeing our thoughts and emotions and changing how we respond to them. We may gradually teach ourselves to focus on the here and now, to be more aware of our thoughts and reactions to the environment around us.

1. Be mindful of your emotions and thoughts

We are urged to let go of the notion that we have any control over our thoughts and emotions via the practice of mindfulness. Instead, it encourages us to pay attention and develop our capacity for emotion. You may better regulate the influence that emotions have on your behavior by being aware of the ups and downs of your thinking.

In this sense, mindfulness is a method of control. The voice in your brain is not always to be believed as you become more conscious of your emotions and how you react to them. One of the biggest steps in regaining control over how ideas and emotions might affect your behavior is realizing that sometimes your thoughts are unhelpful and that they don't have to guide your actions.

2. Concentrate on the now

One may access mindfulness at any time and from any location. An important technique for developing a mindful state is to keep your focus on the here and now. Because tranquillity and peace of mind are most likely to be found here, it is important to keep the mind in the present. It is also the place where our focus is sharpest and where we may be most in touch with our emotions, thoughts, and bodily sensations.

3. Act to bring about change.

It takes work to become aware of your thoughts and emotions as well as to teach your mind to concentrate on the here and now. But the more you do it, the better you'll become, and the outcome might significantly affect your well-being. Our last action-related suggestion is to start your trip by setting up some attainable objectives. A certain approach to being motivated to take action and make great changes in your life is to think about where you want your life to go and the kind of person you want to become.

Last word

It might seem tough to push back against a culture that teaches you that you are in control of your emotions. It may also result in feelings of guilt for having uncontrollable thoughts and emotions, as well as a desire to repress them. An essential first step in directing your energy and attention in the proper direction is realizing that there are aspects of your life that you can influence.

Five

Can Infidelity Ruin a Marriage?

⚜

T his question has no correct or wrong responses. This is so because every relationship is unique and consists of two distinct individuals. While some people see infidelity as a non-negotiable and solid justification for divorce or separation, others believe they can find a way to make it work.

The reality is that while some relationships can survive infidelity, others cannot. You are in the greatest position to assess your connection and decide if you want to continue or end it.

According to data on divorce, marital therapy was required for the majority of infidelities-free marriages. After the fact, a marital counselor serves as a mediator to assist them in making wise choices. Within five years of extramarital relationships, 53% of marriages end in divorce, according to the American Psychological Association.

Only around half of couples who seek assistance can fully recover from one partner's infidelity and continue to be married for more than five years. According to the study, after visiting a marital therapist for six months, the majority of couples see an improvement in their relationship. However, with time, these favorable outcomes diminish, which can then end in divorce.

These statistics demonstrate how often marriages end in divorce when one spouse has an affair, deterring the majority of couples from making an effort to save their union. But this does not imply that a marriage can never withstand adultery, as some claim.

Here's how to know when to leave after infidelity if you're having trouble deciding whether to attempt to salvage your marriage or end it.

Important Things to Think About Before Leaving After Infidelity;

1. The standard of your partnership

Any relationship's quality relies on the couple's history, which may be utilized to decide whether or not to attempt to mend it after adultery. If your relationship has been satisfying for a while, it could be a good idea to first look into the affair to see why your spouse cheated.

On the other hand, if your spouse has cheated on you consistently throughout your relationship, it is more difficult to save the relationship since it is probable that the infidelity will continue.

2. Involvement of emotions

After infidelity, it is best to think about your emotional participation in the situation before determining whether to leave or remain. After having an affair, how you feel about your spouse might influence your choice. It could be wise for you to move away if the love has been replaced by ignorance, indifference, or hurt.

3. The dating history of the unfaithful partner

It is often said that patterns are reliable. Has your boyfriend ever cheated on you? Do they have a history of betraying trust in every relationship? You should be aware that you are in a relationship with a serial cheater who is likely to cheat again if you answer "yes" to both questions.

On the other hand, if your spouse is betraying you for the first time, it may indicate serious problems in your marriage. In some cases, dealing with these problems and reestablishing trust can help you stop cheating in your relationship.

4. The response of the cheating partner

Making decisions based on how your partner acts after they cheat can be beneficial. Do they express regret for their actions and regret? Are they devoted to making sure it never occurs again? Are they still in touch with the cheating partner? Do they intend to seek out the support they will need to resolve their problems? These are all significant elements that may aid you in making the best choice for both your relationship and yourself.

5. Knowing When to Leave After Infidelity

Most people start looking for important warning signs in the relationship that can make walking away from the situation easier when they learn that their spouse has been cheating. Here are warning signs that a marriage or relationship is about to end and when to leave after infidelity.

6. Your spouse won't accept accountability for their deeds

It might be best to end the relationship if your partner refuses to own up to their infidelity and instead places the blame on you and gaslights. You should view this as a red flag that your partner may be a narcissist and that you should expect certain things from them in the future if you decide to stay. Most narcissistic cheating partners shift the blame and claim that you are to blame for their wandering by stressing them out, being disrespectful, inattentive, or unavailable to them.

7. They won't express regret

The cheating partner must be ready to apologize for their actions for the relationship to begin to mend after infidelity. It may be a sign that you are in a toxic relationship and it is best to end it if they won't admit wrongdoing and apologize for it. You have no reason to think the affair won't happen again in the future if they can't find the time to apologize. The best way to protect yourself might be to leave.

8. They won't accept assistance.

One of a happy marriage's greatest assets is marriage counseling. After having an affair, if your spouse refuses to go to a marriage counselor, it might be a sign that they don't want to save the marriage. Without counseling, it becomes even more difficult to get through this challenging time in your relationship. If a couple does not seek counseling after an affair, they typically divorce.

9. You experience stress from attempting to mend the relationship.

Making a relationship work after infidelity can be exhausting and numbing for the betrayed partner. It might be time to think about leaving if you are sick of trying to mend relationships all the time. You've probably had enough if you feel that the relationship is no longer important to you.

They continue to communicate with their partner.

If your partner is still in contact with the person they cheated with, even though they may be sorry and willing to make changes to the relationship, you should take this as a warning sign. If they are still in contact, they will most likely rekindle their relationship and resume their affair. It might be best for you to leave.

10. Missing intimacy

Since this aids in the healing process after infidelity, the majority of cheating spouses will make an effort to reestablish intimacy in their committed relationship. If you still struggle to have a close relationship with your partner, there may be a lack of trust and attraction as a result of the affair. It might be best to break up if you can't get back to being intimate.

Six

How To Prevent Stress In Your Relationship

How does your partnership typically work? You and your partner probably get along well and can succeed as a team. What transpires, however, when something goes wrong and either one of you—or both of you—start to feel freaked out? What are the effects of stress on relationships and what can you do to fortify your marriage against the inescapable stresses of life?

The strongest ties may suffer from relationship stress. When you start to feel that "my relationship is stressing me out," there is a chance that you and your spouse may grow apart, have a dispute, or otherwise lose contact. However, by consistently supporting your spouse while they are under stress, you'll not only learn how to handle stress in relationships but also develop a new level of closeness that draws you two closer together.

AWARENESS OF RELATIONSHIP STRESS

Although managing relationship tension is never simple, it is a necessary aspect of life. Even if your spouse has always been the support in your relationship, there will come a moment when their reserves are depleted, and you will have the chance to offer them the love and encouragement they need. While it could be challenging for you to support your spouse when they're under pressure, doing so will not only foster comfort and connection but also a strong, reliable foundation for the relationship that both parties can depend on.

HOW DO RELATIONSHIPS GET IMPACTED BY STRESS?

Perhaps "How does stress not harm relationships?" would be a better question. According to research, stress may negatively impact our relationships in a variety of ways. People tend to become disoriented, reclusive, and less loving when they are under a lot of stress. The neglect of leisure pursuits results in estrangement from social circles, including one's spouse.

Stress makes us exhibit our worst characteristics. We lack cognitive resources, which causes us to be too watchful and sensitive to criticism. Since we're more irritated, we're more likely to argue over things we'd typically overlook. If relationship stress was already a problem, external stresses will make it 10 times worse.

Men and women respond to relationship stress differently. Stress affects men and women in various ways. Variations in stress hormones are one of the main causes of this. The chemicals cortisol and epinephrine, which are released by the body in response to stress, increase blood pressure and elevate blood sugar levels. The brain then releases oxytocin, which reduces the effects of cortisol and epinephrine by calming emotions.

Men have a higher response to cortisol and epinephrine when they are anxious than women do because men generate less oxytocin during stressful situations.

According to research that appeared in Psychological Review, this made women more inclined to cope with stress by "tending and befriending," or caring individuals around them in an attempt to safeguard both themselves and their offspring. Men, however, emit less oxytocin than women do, which increases their propensity to react to stress by either suppressing their feelings and fleeing the situation or fighting back.

CONSCIOUSNESS OF RELATIONSHIP STRESS

How does your spouse behave under pressure? Our daily obligations and hectic schedules make it simple for us to become lost in our worlds. However, when we fail to notice our partner's stress, we stop connecting and speaking with them. For this reason, it's crucial to go above and above to spot signs that your spouse is anxious.

How does stress impact relationships? will be addressed. first self-examination question: "How does my relationship express stress? How do their eating, sleeping, and emotional patterns affect their energy levels or disposition?

It may be more challenging to interpret a male experiencing high levels of stress since women are more likely than men to express bodily symptoms linked to stress.

By keeping an open line of communication with your spouse, you'll discover chances to show your love and support for them while also strengthening your bond. Learning how to manage your stress and relationships can help you both in the long term.

EFFECTS OF RELATIONSHIP STRESS ON HEALTH

Did you realize that the strain of relationships may make you ill? There is simply too much stress in your relationship if you start experiencing physical or mental health symptoms in addition to "My relationship is stressing me out." Relationship strain may result in mental health issues such as:

- feeling uneasy with your spouse
- excessive scrutiny of your relations
- having trouble controlling your emotions
- feeling distant or depressed
- difficulty sleeping
- Stress in relationships has also been linked in studies to issues with physical health.

According to one research, ambivalent relationships, in which your partner's behaviors with you fluctuate greatly from supportive to antagonistic, are even more detrimental to your physical health than wholly bad ones.

Similar to other types of stress, relationship stress has detrimental impacts on one's health:

- stomach problems
- Skin conditions
- heart disease risk is now more likely
- elevated blood pressure
- weakened immunity
- It's important to consider how stress impacts your physical and mental health in addition to how it affects relationships.

28

MANAGING YOUR STRESS

If you have difficulties controlling your stress, you won't be much assistance to your spouse. Stress may rapidly build up while you're occupied with the regular tasks of life if you're not aware of your thoughts and emotions. One of the most effective stress-reduction techniques you can master is relaxation. You may lessen your relationship tension when you learn to regulate your emotions and relax. Here are some methods for managing oneself in terms of relationships and stress.

CREATE A PEACEFUL SETTING

Stress often develops when you're attempting to get through the day with little sleep or food. Aim to slow down and carve out time for your body rather than pushing through. Before night, turn off all gadgets to create a quiet space where you can sleep well. A warm bath or a good book may assist the mind to relax and reduce tension before going to bed.

INVEST IN YOUR BODY

Relationships, stress, and physiology are all interconnected. Replace coffee and any other sugary beverages with natural juices or water while you're at work. A well-hydrated body can handle stress better. Ensure that you are providing your body with the correct kind of fuel, including a balanced diet rich in whole foods, lean protein, and a variety of vegetables and super foods. Find an activity you love doing; exercise may help you relax and clear your brain. You take care of your body and mind simultaneously when you look after them.

Set yourself first

There are additional things you may do to look after your mind. Self-care and relaxation are important components of stress management in relationships. Try yoga, which is uplifting and calming, or meditate to clear your mind. Use massage, calming music, aromatherapy, or other integrative medicine techniques. When you are relaxed, you can better manage tension and conflict in your relationship

Seven

How to Heal a Relationship and Forgive a Cheater

While some individuals would never pardon a cheater, others might if they made a sincere attempt at repentance. Regardless, it's never simple to mend a relationship after such events.

It requires a lot of work, trust, candor, and shared empathy.

This book will examine the psychology of adultery and relationship repair. You'll understand how to forgive a cheater and if it's feasible after the article. Let's get started.

Knowing The Causes Of Cheating

We need to comprehend why individuals cheat to learn how to forgive them for cheating.

What comes first? Why would a spouse betray you? Others claim they were searching for something that was lacking from the relationship, while others make excuses for themselves by stating they were simply having a weak moment and making a mistake.

But what's this? That is all untrue. People intentionally lie. Honesty is the first step in healing a relationship. Only when the cheater comes clean and admits what they did can the relationship start to mend.

The worst thing someone can do after making a mistake is to rationalize their actions or victimize themselves. Having stated that, what is the other partner's perspective?

The effects of adultery on the other person

If you're asking yourself, "Should you forgive a cheater?" you need to consider how it will impact both you and the other person.

In addition to the hurt and betrayal the individual experiences, their sense of value and self-worth may also suffer. Since infidelity may shock you and your relationship, some individuals may even experience symptoms of post-traumatic stress disorder (PTSD).

It's possible for other mental health issues, such as sadness or anxiety, to develop or worsen. No one ever shakes their head and continues living their life without feeling resentment or disappointment, therefore infidelity always has negative effects.

How To Reconcile With A Cheater And Forgive Them

Here are some suggestions you may take into account if you have determined that you should forgive a cheater and wish to improve your relationship. Here are some guidelines you might use if you're concerned about how to forgive someone who cheated:

1. Take some time to contemplate your emotions.

You may not be ready to forgive just yet.

   You could experience strong feelings like grief, anger, betrayal, and worry, but that's good and natural. Make sure to spend some time with your sentiments without passing judgment on them. The first step to letting go is to accept what we've gone through.

   Which area of your body becomes active when you experience anxiety? Breathe deeply and keep your attention there. Pay close attention since your body has a lot more to tell you than you would imagine.

2. Have a protracted, responsible discussion

You and your spouse need to get coffee or take a seat on the sofa to talk about what transpired after things have returned to normal and have calmed down. Tell them how you feel and go through the infidelity before and after.

3. Establish limits

Even more so after betrayal, boundaries are necessary for any healthy partnership. The victim of the cheating should impose additional restrictions since they now have more trust problems and worry, while the cheater is also entitled to their views.

Consider the following while establishing boundaries:

- What is acceptable to me and what is not? Can one partner flirt with a male or a girl, for instance, or is it insulting to me?
- How can I verify that you are telling the truth without being intrusive or

controlling?

- What actions may the cheater use to demonstrate remorse, a desire to improve, and a desire to make things right?
- Can I let the other person go out and have a good time without worrying about them?
- Boundaries may become invasive or even harmful. It's better to decide what you are prepared to put up with and what is off-limits as a group. Although it may be difficult to win back your partner's trust, this is no justification for controlling and manipulating them.
- On trust, relationships are created. If you have to watch your partner's every action, you don't trust them, which means you're probably not ready to move on and forgive them.

4. Strike a balance in your private life.

When should you pardon a liar? Quite simply, whenever you feel like doing it.

Relationships may often consume a lot of our time without us even realizing it, particularly when dealing with a scenario like this one jointly.

Don't forget to give yourself some time. Concentrate on your profession, socialize with friends, visit relatives, indulge in hobbies, etc. Finding yourself again is the first step toward recovery since coping with infidelity may cause you to lose your confidence and self-worth.

seek out other people's emotional support. You don't have to do it alone; your buddies are here to support you.

5. Attend couple's counseling

You may get therapeutic guidance from a relationship professional. They will reveal feelings and ideas you weren't aware of having.

We can do it on our own! may cause you to reject this alternative, but there is no need to be concerned since therapists are used to dealing with circumstances like these.

Find a person with whom you feel both at ease and make sure they don't exhibit any favoritism—that might be more detrimental than anything else. It may generate imbalance by giving one partner the idea that they are more correct or wrong than the other.

When both spouses are ready to examine each other and their relationship, couples counseling may be beneficial.

Typical Sexual Issues Therapists for Couples Hear Frequently

In a perfect world, every sexual encounter would be trouble-free. Unfortunately, it is not how things operate in reality. Many issues may occur while you're getting down to business, as any couple's therapist will attest to. Fortunately, they offer solutions for the following 8 problems, allowing you to enjoy the finest sex imaginable.

1. "My thoughts won't stay in one place."
   The co-director of Integrative Therapy of Greater Washington, Julie Bindeman, Psy.D., tells SELF that her female clients often complain that they are too preoccupied to engage in sex. This is particularly true for many mothers since having children may make it difficult to have any erotic ideas. Scheduling sex can seem contradictory, but it could be beneficial. "You may be better equipped to adapt to something when you know it's going to happen,"

adds Bindeman. Additionally, adding some variety via toys or fresh sex positions helps keep you focused.

2. "I can't be warm and fuzzy because I'm a male."

The notion that men are emotionless, sex-obsessed robots does them no favors. According to Gary Brown, Ph.D., a marital and family therapist with a license in Los Angeles, "the males frequently feel like they're bound by this concept that they're emotional Neanderthals" when we speak to couples in our practice. Many people confess that they truly want to feel more connected outside of the bedroom, but they simply aren't sure how. By being open about your own emotions and encouraging a monkey to see what, the monkey does dynamic, you may make it simpler for him. When he does get gooey, you may also show him, additional love—positive reinforcement is key.

3. "I have to start things off."

Resentment might develop if one person feels that the other doesn't make the good times roll sufficiently. What About Me? author and marital and sex therapist Jane Greer, Ph.D., of New York, says, "You can do it instead when you're in the mood. Instead of waiting for your spouse to initiate and feeling disappointed when it doesn't happen. Tell yourself to stop letting selfishness ruin your relationships. And if you're on the receiving end of the equation, realize that your spouse is asking for you to initiate sex more often because they want to feel wanted, therefore complying with their request can greatly strengthen your relationship.

4. "Where did the foreplay go?"

This story may have been told during happy hour around the table, and if it pertains to you, you are aware of how aggravating it may be. When you're in the heat of the moment, Fran Walfish, Psy.D., a Beverly Hills child, parenting, and relationship psychotherapist and co-star of WE tv's Sex Box, advises SELF, "it's ideal to physically show your spouse what feels wonderful to you by putting their hand in the proper locations." When speaking up, it might be good to phrase your request favorably, such as "I love it so much when you do XYZ." In this manner, it seems less critical and more supportive of what people currently do.

5. "I wish we showed each other more, love."

Fortunately, there is an enjoyable solution for this. Nikki Martinez, Psy.D., a therapist in Chicago and a Telehealth counselor for Betterhelp.com, advises SELF, "Each day you should tell each other one thing you admire about the other person." Martinez suggests including the simple gestures you likely used to express love when you first began dating, such as holding hands, wrapping your arms around each other while sitting together, caressing each other's shoulders, and the like if that seems too formulaic for your tastes.

6. "There is a gap in our emotional connection."

The situation becomes more complicated if one person wants an emotional connection but isn't experiencing it, even while it's OK if both parties are just interested in the physical release. Brown refers to this as "empty sex," which doesn't sound alluring. Work on building closeness outside of the bedroom to help dispel this sense. Spend more time with your spouse, look for new things you can do together that will strengthen your relationship, and find out what makes you both happy in different ways, advises Brown.

7. "There is crazy pressure to have a kid."

The male in a straight marriage may feel like he is acting while they are trying to become pregnant. According to Bindeman, "there should be a balance between expressing when you're ovulating and spontaneity." Finding the right balance requires open communication since some male partners want to be informed about every aspect of their cycle while others would like to be less informed. No matter where he ends up, you two may revive the thrill of sex even if the result is conception. Wearing undergarments and sending erotic SMS, for example, might make having a kid feel more like joy than a duty, according to Bindeman.

8. "My lover refuses to engage in oral sex."

If your spouse won't engage in oral sex despite your desire, you could feel rejected. Greer claims that after that, you become upset and dissatisfied and are likely to stop wanting to have sex. Ask your spouse to consider it as something they can do sometimes to demonstrate their interest in your satisfaction if they aren't a big lover of oral sex but you truly appreciate it. According to Greer, "giving a little goes a long way toward making your spouse feel cared for."

Eight

Seven (7) Pointers for Rebuilding Trust After Infidelity in a Relationship

R elationships may be destroyed by infidelity, and for some people, there is just no turning back after one spouse has been dishonest. However, if you and your partner don't want your relationship to end, you both need to be capable of returning to the previous state. Make sure you're doing all you can to move on because if you don't follow these steps, learning how to rebuild trust after infidelity will be challenging, if not impossible.

1. Discuss it

The first step is that you must discuss it with someone. Get everything on the table so that your spouse is aware of what transpired. Was the infidelity a brief slip-up or a sustained affair? This will be significant for certain partners. Was there more than one individual involved in the adultery throughout time, or was it just one? How long did this last? Was there a complete emotional connection or was it only a physical one? Some partners may find this to be essential as well. It can be crucial to talk about if there was any physical closeness or whether the infidelity was exclusively emotional.

2. Be frank and truthful

Both sides must be absolutely honest and transparent while discussing issues as part of the conversation. If the relationship lasted a long period, you must own up to it. You must be honest about any prior relationships you may have had. Some individuals think they must admit what they have done to keep their spouse from leaving them. In actuality, your spouse has to be fully aware of everything. They are more likely to leave if they don't when they learn later. At least having all the information at once makes it simpler for the two of you to decide what to do next.

3. Let everything out

You shouldn't discuss anything else throughout this conversation. Once you've gone through everything and the person who was cheated on has asked all of their questions, it has to be done, even if it takes a few days, weeks, or many therapy sessions. This calls for careful consideration of what it is you need to know or want to know to set your mind at ease. You must express to them your feelings and what all of this means to you. Rebuilding trust in a relationship requires the other person to have a better awareness of the fact that you won't be able to fully trust them right away.

4. Set the Conditions

Rules could be necessary for both parties to feel secure and trustworthy enough to proceed. The victim of the cheating may wish to lay out expectations for their spouse in terms of openness, friendships, and other areas. There may be even more caution or "rules" surrounding engagement with that person, particularly by one party alone, if the person with whom the affair occurred will be involved in your life in any manner—personally, professionally, or in any other way.

5. Leave It Behind

The infidelity ought to be in the past after you and your spouse have discussed everything and chosen to go on with your relationship. As a result, neither spouse may bring it up again. The cheating partner is not permitted to bring up the relationship to exert pressure on the other person. While things don't go the way they want them to or when the two of you are arguing, the cheater is not permitted to bring it up as a threat. The affair must be fully behind you.

6. Assign blame appropriately

It does not indicate that there is a problem with you if you have been cheated on. Many individuals believe that if they hadn't done something improperly, their spouse wouldn't have cheated on them. That is not the situation. Your spouse is to fault for what transpired. They bear full responsibility for it since they decided to have a connection of any kind with someone who is not a member of your partnership. That entails not holding you accountable for whatever you did or did not do. Moreover, they must refrain from pointing the finger at the cheating partner for any actions or inactions.

7. Seek expert assistance

When you have experienced infidelity in a relationship, it may be difficult to get over the feelings that come with it. Trusting yourself or your spouse may be challenging. It might be challenging to avoid making too many assumptions about each contact they have with others. By seeking professional assistance, you may both work through what occurred on your own and as a couple, enabling you to move on in your relationship in a healthy way and leave the past behind.

Nine

Five (5) Important Steps in Recovery from Infidelity

ndeed, getting over an affair will probably be one of the toughest things you ever have to do. Similarly, you can have second thoughts about your choice to remain together while you go through the healing process. On the other hand, you can emerge from adultery with a stronger, deeper bond between you.

Of course, it would be much preferable to skip the path to healing and rehabilitation after infidelity completely, but here you are. You are now dealing with betrayal, shattered trust, and the loss of the connection you believed you had. Is it possible for couples to mend after something like this, you think as you choose whether to remain together or split.

The journey ahead will be filled with hiccups, heartbreak, and sadness, yet it may lead you to the place where reassurance and reconnection are found. Let's discuss the five most important steps in the recovery from infidelity.

1. You've now fully disclosed yourself.

The deceived spouse will feel helpless following the affair; they lack knowledge and will be left wondering what transpired.

They might even develop an obsession with the turn of events. When relying solely on conjecture, the imagination might run wild.

Agree to meet and discuss what transpired when the first shock of the news has subsided. You should both be prepared because this will be a challenging conversation.

But it must be completed.

It's time to disclose everything completely. The perpetrator must explain what transpired to the betrayed spouse, and the guilty people must be given a chance to clear their names.

2. Empathize with one another.

Both parties will experience temporary regret. So how can one move past an affair? The spouse who was cheated on will undoubtedly feel betrayed and even denigrated; but, the spouse who cheated is also likely to experience a flurry of emotions, including shame and regret for the wrongs committed. And both partners will be lamenting what their union once was. Both spouses must show compassion for one another to recover from this infidelity. Each of them must likewise resist the want to wallow in their misery. They both feel awful about what has occurred to them, that much is true. But remember the other person's emotions.

It will be simpler for both of you to recover from your troubling sentiments the more you can concentrate on what the other person is experiencing.

3. Express regret and accept accountability

Each party involved has to hear the other's apology, no matter how difficult the words may be to utter. The person who cheated should express their regret for the affair in a way that the other spouse may be certain of their sincerity.

But it's also important for both partners to discuss and express regret for the factors that contributed to the marriage's current state.

Then, to go on, they must each accept the other's regrets, even if it takes some time to do so. Then, both partners must accept responsibility for any wrongdoing connected to the infidelity.

4. Choose to remain together or not.

Do the two of you remain in love? Where things will proceed from here basically revolves around this question. Even a little amount of affection is sufficient.

You may opt to proceed jointly. Naturally, you can't compel the other spouse to remain; all you have authority over is what you decide to do. Hence, discuss it.

What kind of life would you lead if you remained together? You may develop a closer relationship if you stuck together. Just be careful to discuss so you both understand where the situation will go from here.

5. Reinstate faith in your marriage.

It's time to begin rebuilding once you are at zero. Accept that things will change and continue to be dedicated to making it work. Unfortunately, if you want to get beyond infidelity, you have to retrace your steps. But instead of seeing it as a nuisance, see it as an opportunity. First, it's time to speak with a marital therapist.

You need a third person to assist you to speak through your feelings and the crucial concerns that may arise. It takes courage to rebuild trust since it necessitates facing your most vulnerable sides. Together, you can overcome this if you commit to supporting each other through it.

What Leads to Adultery?

Infidelity is one of the few issues in a relationship that may break hearts and destroy relationships. The obvious inquiry after such a finding is "why?"

There are several factors at play when one partner decides to violate their trust agreement. For instance, there may be

- communication difficulties
- broken connection
- failing to meet each other's requirements
- addiction
- mental illness problems
- Issues with physical health
- absence of love, attachment, or concern for one another
- Although their explanation may not support their decision, it may provide some insight into the path to healing you both must take.

Finding out about your partner's infidelity may completely rock your life. Therefore, it's crucial to look for assistance. You may wish to get in touch with a reliable friend, family member, or religious authority. It could also be essential to get expert therapy.

In the next chapter we would be discussing some crucial actions to do to aid your recovery from infidelity.

Ten

How to Continue After Infidelity

The relationship specialist Dr. John Gottman is well known for his work. He also created the Trust Revival Method, a successful strategy for dealing with infidelity. Dr. Margaret Rutherford is an author for the Gottman Institute and has a long list of accomplishments. Here, she gives "Science-Based Steps to Heal from an Affair" using Dr. Gottman's approach. She offers some suggestions:

1. Seek couples counseling. She emphasizes that individual therapy might make the recovery process more difficult. Instead, couples counseling offers a setting where couples may focus on being open with one another and rebuilding trust.

Get ready to learn more about the tale later. As the two of you work through the complicated emotions that come with adultery, the full truth is likely to come out. There are several explanations for why this is. For instance, there may be self-preservation, defensiveness, embarrassment, fury, fear, and sadness between the two of you.

2. Recognize that the relationship has to be fixed in certain areas. That spouse is the only one who can decide whether to have an affair. Similarly, for the

relationship to improve, both of you must adapt.

3. Establish clear guidelines for talking about the affair. Couples may find it difficult to effectively communicate alone due to the grief of betrayal. Instead, think about establishing strong rules for these interactions. It could be wise to hold off until you are with your therapist, for instance. Setting a time limit and deciding to end the conversation if it isn't moving forward is useful if you must speak sooner. After all, these discussions may easily escalate into an explosive situation.

4. Forgiveness. Forgiveness is a key component of recovery after infidelity. The person who betrayed trust must first actively seek and strive for pardon. You will also need to at some time provide unreserved forgiveness.

It is true that after an affair, a couple may recover and even find a deeper connection. The procedure might be difficult and time-consuming.

It will be crucial as you advance to learn how to interact with one another effectively. You may practice and use more meaningful discussions with EFT treatment. The ability to reestablish and restore the trust required for success may also be learned.

Eleven

Fifteen (15) Ways to Mend a Damaged Relationship

Contrary to what some may say, dancing in the flames of a burned bridge is a terrific motivator to work harder and keep moving ahead. Burning bridges is a great method to stay up with the rat race. Unfortunately, there are instances when it is necessary to reconstruct a destroyed bridge to further the greater good. Here are some strategies for mending a damaged relationship.

1. Start a cordial and friendly conversation.

A brief invitation or a simple "Hi" is sufficient to start a discussion. Depending on how they blocked you, you may also need to indicate who you are in addition to the fact that you sent them a message. This is all that has to be stated; refrain from saying anything further (or sending more than one message in total) until they react. Otherwise, you'll come out as irritable.

2. State Your Intentions Clearly.

Once a discourse has begun, take advantage of it by being upfront, direct, and honest about your goals. This will demonstrate your regard for the other person and aid in mending the previously damaged trust. Never assume that someone can read your mind since, in reality, no one can, no matter how hard you concentrate on communicating ideas.

3. The power of love.

You're trying to mend a damaged connection because you either need something from them or care about them. Even if you need something, put the other person's needs before your own. He or she will be more willing to assist you if you demonstrate your concern for them.

4. Construct a Bridge and Move On.

Put aside all of your old problems since they belong in the past. You may talk about the problems you encountered in your last relationship attempt, but concentrating on them will only make matters worse. Close the distance between the two of you and quickly heal your rift.

5. Be Sincere (In a Nice Way).

Be truthful at all times, even when you disagree. Your relationship may not have been damaged by deceit, but it won't be restored by deceit either. Just be careful not to come across as defensive or offensive, and if you can't keep it polite, don't say anything.

6. Idea-generation

Get the other person involved in your efforts to mend your connection. Put the onus on them and request their participation since, if he or she is talking, he or she is at least interested in hearing what you have to say.

7. Hands-off command

Always keep in mind to separate oneself from life's outcomes. If you place all your trust in this person, their rejection will break you. Instead, identify who you are and how you respond, but don't hold out hope for the perfect outcome.

8. Express regret.

Few disputes in life cannot be addressed with an apology. Even if the other person isn't interested, it will at the very least offer you the chance to forget about what happened and go on.

9. Assume accountability.

Regardless of whether you think you were at fault, you should always take responsibility. Accepting responsibility can help you close the perceived gap between you and the other person, who fervently feels you are.

10. Keep from pressing buttons.

Keep in mind that you and the other person dislike one another (or at least used to). You are aware that certain triggers affect that individual; act like an adult and resist the need to press those buttons.

11. Be optimistic.

Always try to think positively about life. Even if something doesn't work out, you may look forward to the next opportunity. Keep forward-focused so that you may project appealing confidence to others. The other person will be intrigued by this and start to question why they don't know you.

12. Be Honest.

No matter what occurs, always be true to yourself. Instead of succeeding as someone else, you would want to fail your way. You'd be shocked at how much honesty will help you in life; don't waste your time trying to be what the other person wants since it's not a game.

13. Be Firm About Your Limits.

You should be treated with respect since you have personal limits and make an effort to respect those of others. When someone crosses a limit you've set, be careful to remind them in a courteous and understanding manner. But make sure it's one you both agree on so you don't accuse somebody unfairly of crossing a border they weren't aware existed.

14. Continue to lead the conversation.

Try to steer the discussion toward your objectives regardless of where it goes. Invite the other person to a future meeting or talk if the interaction is going well. Otherwise, ask him or her for whatever it was you first contacted them for.

15. You Need to Let Go Occasionally.

It's possible that the other person just doesn't want to reconnect, despite your best efforts. Forget about it if they don't answer or come off as hostile. There are billions of individuals in the world, therefore there is no justification for wasting your time on someone you don't like.

It is challenging to mend a broken relationship because both parties must confront the resentment and mistrust that caused the breakup in the first place. Reconnect with the individual by text, email, or online if you want to mend a strained connection from the past. They could be intrigued if he or she replies. If not, you now have the satisfaction you need to proceed.

The Demise of Your Relationship Due to Deceit

When the subject of adultery makes it into our daily media diet, we can claim to have seen it coming or we might respond in astonishment. In any case, we don't exactly turn our heads. We pick up information, identities, sources, and suspicions without even intending to. The majority of us would agree that it serves little use to speculate on the specifics, agreements, falsehoods, details, and circumstances of a stranger's affair; nonetheless, our preoccupation with others' transgressions should reveal something about ourselves and the environment we live in.

It's difficult to dispute that there is a lot about the ethics of our interactions that needs to be reviewed as a society. According to a 2002 research that was published in the Journal of Couple & Relationship Therapy, 45 to 55 percent of married women and 50 to 60 percent of married men in the United States have extramarital sex at some point in their relationship.

However, according to other research, 90% of Americans think adultery is ethically unacceptable. Although it is often disapproved of, infidelity is unquestionably common. Given this contrast, it is critical for every couple to discuss how they will handle the topic of fidelity as well as to assess the degree of openness and honesty in their union.

The most harmful component of adultery may be deception. Lies and deception undermine people's faith in the accuracy of their perceptions and subjective experiences. The deceived party learns shockingly and painfully that the person they have been engaged with has a hidden existence and that there is a side of their spouse that they were unaware of as a result of the breach of trust brought on by a partner's covert contact with another person.

It is wrong to interfere with someone else's perception of reality. Going to tremendous measures to mislead someone might make them doubt their sanity, but hiding a very little secret from someone you're close to reduces that person's reality. While it's true that experiencing attraction or falling in love may be beyond our control, we do have control over whether we act on those feelings. Being open and sincere about our actions is essential to building a relationship with genuine substance.

We are taught as children that lying is bad, but as we age, the boundaries seem to blur more and more. This is particularly true when we are dealing with the difficult circumstances that come along with personal relationships. We mistakenly change ourselves to "make it work" all too often when we get intimate with someone. We struggle to break away from damaging behaviors and unhealthy connecting styles that deform both ourselves and our relationships because of the heavy emotional baggage we carry from the past. When this occurs, we may sabotage and abuse our relationships out of jealousy, possessiveness, insecurity, and mistrust. We no longer live in the reality of what the relationship is but in the fiction of what we believe a relationship should be once it becomes about surrendering ourselves or rejecting who we are.

A woman whose partner becomes so envious that he bans her from being alone with other guys may serve as an illustration of this. Another scenario would have a guy with a spouse who has to continuously be reminded of his love and desire for her because she feels so insecure. Even though these couples may continue acting as if everything is OK, they will probably start to feel resentment against one another and lose interest in the union. Dishonesty may flourish in these kinds of constrained circumstances. The guy may fabricate an attraction he is beginning to feel for another woman, while the woman may fabricate time she spent alone with a male acquaintance or coworker.

We are being genuine to ourselves and our relationships when we treat them with respect and candor. We may choose how to spend our life and what we do without sacrificing our morality or behaving out of duty or guilt. Restricting our partners may affect their feeling of energy and unintentionally pave the way for dishonesty. This is not to indicate that individuals shouldn't expect their partners to be devoted; rather, it means that partners should make an effort to keep the lines of communication about their emotions and their relationship open and honest.

We may just be able to trust our partners enough to believe them when they claim they won't act on this desire if they trust us enough to acknowledge that they find someone else appealing. Our relationships become cleaner and more durable the more open we are with one another. On the other hand, when we get used to holding secrets, we are more prone to fabricate ever-larger falsehoods.

Twelve

MICRO CHEATING

The phrase "micro-cheating" is used to describe actions that aren't often seen as "real infidelity," but exhibit certain characteristics of it, such as dishonesty and secrecy while in a committed relationship. Even though they may appear insignificant or simple to ignore, these things may nonetheless harm your relationship with your significant other. You can spot micro-infidelity and deal with it if it happens in your relationship by having a thorough awareness of what it looks like and what matters.

Why Would You Micro Cheat?

Micro Cheating is the term used to describe little, improper activities that take place outside of a committed relationship and are often done accidentally. Since there is no sexual activity involved, many individuals would not consider these activities to constitute infidelity; yet, micro-cheating can violate a couple's unwritten or expressed standards, trust, and boundaries in other ways. Even if a small-scale affair isn't necessarily the consequence of micro-cheating, future relationship issues may arise as a result.

Cheating vs Micro-Cheating

While the term "infidelity" may have many various interpretations depending on the person, most relationship experts agree that it refers to any action that is concealed or causes betrayal emotions in a committed partnership. While a physical affair and micro-cheating have something in common, typical physical infidelity generally includes more sexual and physical elements than micro-cheating does. Micro cheating is harder to see and characterize than traditional cheating.

Emotional Vs Small-Scale Cheating

When a person covertly has an intimate, non-sexual connection with someone who isn't their spouse, such behavior is known as emotional infidelity. Microcheating, or little activities like sharing private information with a crush or having a casual lunch with an ex, may lead to emotional affairs. However, if committed frequently, these minor transgressions have the potential to develop into more serious offenses like emotional or physical adultery.

Examples of Small-Scale Fraud

If you're unsure if contacting your ex or going out with your crush for drinks constitutes micro-cheating, consider the following: Do I keep important facts from my spouse regularly? Can my actions harm them or the relationship in any way? What if the positions were reversed? How would I feel? Your responses could provide light on whether or not micro-cheating is taking place by showing if these behaviors cause emotions of pain and betrayal.

A few instances of micro-cheating are 2, 4, 6, and 7.

- flirtatiously messaging or texting someone
- like someone's Instagram or Facebook profile or leaving a provocative remark there
- Online or in person, lying about your relationship status
- maintaining a dating profile to see whether you match with someone "better" than your significant other
- giving a person you know is attracted to you your phone number
- Going over and beyond to appear good so that your crush at work would be impressed Cyberstalking a crush or an ex constantly
- Sexting, discussing your sexual life, or emailing another person nude photos
- Frequent communication with a flirtatious person
- Before going out with friends, take off your wedding or engagement ring.
- the act of flirting with others
- going to happy hour with your employer without telling your spouse
- maintaining frequent contact with a former crush.

Micro Cheating Warning Signs

Microcheating may happen everywhere, including online, at work, and in social settings, but it isn't always obvious. It might be difficult to resist wondering or become suspicious when confronted with any unusual behaviors or actions, including the problems of identifying micro-cheating.

While every circumstance is unique, some typical indications of micro-cheating include:

2,4,5,6,7

Secrecy

Any type of infidelity, even micro-cheating, is often characterized by secrets, lies, and deception. Although wanting privacy is common, concealment might point to more serious problems with faithfulness and trust.

Examples of partner confidentiality include:

Withholding information about the nature of their social media activity (or lying about cheating) or hiding certain information
deleting or hiding texts or emails
taking calls outdoors or whispering
Turning their phone off when they are near their partners
closing their computer abruptly when their significant other enters the room

No attention

When someone is micro-cheating, they may seem disengaged, busy, or as if their thoughts are elsewhere. It may be common for individuals to get distracted sometimes, particularly during busy or trying times, but the constant concern with other things and neglect of a partner raises suspicions of adultery as well as a lack of devotion to the union.

An example of an uncooperative spouse is:

- They regularly gaze at them or are continually using their phone or other gadgets.
- When participating in a date or another couple's activities, they seem disoriented.
- They become emotionally, cognitively, or physically aloof during a heartfelt dialogue They look uninterested or mentally disoriented They disregard the primary connection

Overcoming Relationship Limits

The common definition of micro-cheating and infidelity in general is when one spouse violates the other's expectations of loyalty and trust. Whether they are aware of it or not, those who micro-cheat often breach relationship boundaries. When their spouse has requested them to stop, they could continue to talk to their ex or "like" photographs of models on social media while knowing that doing so makes them uncomfortable. A border, whether spoken or inferred, is often breached.

Five Symptoms of Micro Cheating

Consider thinking about your behavior and looking at your motivations if you think you could be micro-cheating on your partner. Since only you understand your feelings and motivations, you must examine your actions closely and decide if they were improper. The things that directly affect you, your spouse, and your relationship are ultimately what matters the most.

These are some indicators that you could be micro-cheating:

- You're fixated on being online, on your phone, and on social media to give or get attention from beautiful individuals.
- You portray yourself as single both online and in person.
- You often go out with attractive individuals without telling your spouse.
- You may be chatting to an ex or a crush while hiding it from your spouse by adding them to your phone under a fake name.
- You often downplay these actions and how they could affect your primary connection.

The 5 Telltale Signs You're Being Microcheated

Micro-cheating may be hard to detect, but if you suspect anything is going on, it may be helpful to watch for signals of unusual behavior. Your initial inclination may be to confront your spouse right away if you suspect that they are cheating on you. Take stock before acting hastily to see whether your spouse is indeed micro-cheating or if there is a more reasonable explanation for their actions.

You may notice these signs if you're being micro-cheated:

- Your spouse speaks to an ex or a specific individual they have never mentioned before frequently.
- Your significant other looks preoccupied or emotionally distant, neglecting your connection.

- They keep their social media and communication applications private.
- Your spouse doesn't bring up your existence on social media, at work, among their friends, etc.
- When you raise any of these issues, they get hostile, minimize it, or attempt to gaslight you.

Thirteen

Five (5) recommendations for terminating a toxic relationship.

N o matter how unhealthy a relationship is, ending it may be quite hard. Since studies have shown that falling in love stimulates the same brain regions as cocaine usage, some of this may be attributable to fundamental biological factors.

The brains of lovers and cocaine addicts both have increased activity in the dopamine-producing pleasure regions and reduced activity in the frontal lobe, which is where cognition takes place. In other words, although being in love might make us feel wonderful, it can also have a very bad effect on our judgment.

Love is sometimes equated to addiction because of this. Love may have negative side effects like abuse or gaslight, much as addiction. Despite all of these drawbacks, it might be difficult to get rid of romantic attraction and sentiments of love.

If you feel stuck in a relationship that you know is harmful, take into account these 5 recommendations for terminating it permanently:

1. Acknowledge the problem.

Being aware is the first step. Learn what makes a relationship unhealthy, or consider seeing a therapist or counselor. Examine your relationship closely, honestly, and objectively. Be sincere with yourself.

Is the connection I have with this individual serving my best interests?

Has my relationship affected the other areas of my life negatively?

Does this relationship undermine my confidence?

If you answered "yes" to any of these questions, think about ending the relationship or seeking help from a professional.

2. FEEL WHAT YOU WANT

Usually, it's difficult to let go. Even if terminating a relationship was in your best interests, it could not be easy. Instead of attempting to suppress your feelings, honor whatever suffering you may be going through and allow yourself to feel it. Embracing sadness as a necessary component of the journey may aid in your recovery.

3. DISCOVER THE LESSON

Since they feel their time there was squandered, many people who leave a toxic relationship feel regret or humiliation. Nevertheless, everyone that enters our life has something to teach us. Instead of viewing it as time wasted, try to find the relationship's lesson. What have you discovered about this person? What benefits does the cooperation provide you? What adjustments have you made on a personal level, and how may you respond to events differently going forward?

Life lessons sometimes need repeated examination before they are fully comprehended. If you try to find the lesson this relationship taught you, you could be less likely to apply it to new relationships.

4. Establish division.

Putting some distance between yourself and someone you are used to spending a lot of time with may be difficult, but doing so is usually necessary if you want to terminate the connection. This doesn't mean you can't be friends with your ex, but it's usually best to wait until both parties have had some time to heal before making an effort to get together.

5. DESTROY THE MEMORIALS.

It could be tempting to save every souvenir from a previous relationship. However, doing so could prevent you from moving on with your life. You may want to keep any old love letters, gift receipts, photographs, or movie ticket stubs hidden until you're ready to move on.

Fourteen

Conclusion

D o not lash out. Take no revenge. Try harder. Much improved. Climb higher. Become so consumed by your own accomplishment that you lose track of the past. So, if you were cheated on, just keep in mind that there was nothing wrong with you. Avoid wasting your time pursuing retribution. It's not worth it, I promise. Playing games won't help you right now; the only thing that will heal you is directing your energy in a positive direction. Just be mindful of yourself. The rest can wait.

Printed in Great Britain
by Amazon

35429527R00042